Cacophony

Love

[signature]

Copyright © 2006 Elliott Eli Jackson
All rights reserved.
ISBN: 1-4196-4388-6

To order additional copies, please contact us.
BookSurge, LLC
www.booksurge.com
1-866-308-6235
orders@booksurge.com

Cacophony
A Collection of poems

Elliott Eli Jackson

2006

Cacophony

Table of Contents

This Cacophony — xvii

Life

Avant-garde	3
At Face Value	4
Dad's Chair	5
Waiting for Dad	6
Darkness Overcomes Me	7
Earth Crying, Dying	8
Failed Attempt	9
Family Dinner	10
Family Fiber	11
The Grocery List	12
The Periodicals	13
I Left My Mark	14
In Natchez	15
Lean Not On Your Own Understanding	16
Manifesto of Youth	17
Metamorphosis	18
Misunderstood	19
My Heart Went Out That Night! (Roaming Bogotá)	20
Not When It Comes To Momma	22
Separatism	23
Is This Deep or What	24
Shallow Man	25
She Walks the Line	26
Encore	27
Boutique	28

Mad Man	29
The Sun Also Shines	30
The Violin	31
The Artist	32
Volume	33
Thick Lips	34
What Ever Happened to the Milkman?	35
What If Mankind Used The Feminine Side?	36
Why	37

Love

A Voice on the Phone	41
Chivalrous	42
Constrictions	43
Emeralds in Her Eyes	44
South of the Border	45
If You Love Me	46
How Could I Let Her Get Away?	47
How Will You Know?	48
How Many Hearts	49
Sheers at the Window	50
I Saw a Heron	51
If I	52
If Love Comes Your Way	53
Internet Affair	54
The Matchmaker	55
Intellectual	56
It Must Be	57
Keepsake	58
The Shoe	59
Love Me	60
Love Retreat from Me	61
Marry Me!	62
The Answer	63
Matters of the Heart	64
Mental	65
One Million Kisses	66
Out of the Rain	67
Piece de resistance	68
Tormented	69

Post Traumatic Stress	70
Ready	71
Shadows of the Heart	72
She Was a Concubine in Her Mind	73
Sinful	74
Take Me to Mary's Grave	75
That Kiss	76
The Center of My Universe	77
The Garden	78
These Three Things	79
Until The Sun Shines No More	80
While You Were Out	81
Why Won't You Set Me Free?	82
Window Conversation	83
Women	84
You Make My Rivers Flow	85

Spirit

A Storm Is Coming	89
Down on Bended Knees	90
Dreaming	91
Father Said	92
Glacier	93
Midnight Prayer	94
Misty Lake	95
Nomad	96
Plugged In	97
Sleep, Shall I Find Thee?	98
Taking Out Time	99
The Colosseum	100
The Hand of God	101
The Me You Can Not See	102
The Process	103
The Unseen	104
Wandering Souls	105
Well, Well, Well	106
Who Am I?	107
You're Invited	108

Dedicated to
Harold and Florastein Jackson
Shanee and Micah
Elliott, Brandy, Olivia and baby Ava
Lubbie, Harolyn, John and Ramona
Diane Marie

Introduction

Cacophony, according to Webster's Dictionary, is defined as a "discordant and meaningless mixture of different sounds". I chose this title because it clearly reflects the state of mind from which the thoughts and ideas for my poetry are developed. Words that make no sense come in no particular order. I write them down and poems appear. I had not written any poems since childhood. I never thought of poetry and I sure did not ever think I would have a book. Nonetheless, here is my first offering. There will be more to follow. I must give special acknowledgment to Neale Donald Walsch and Oprah Winfrey; unbeknownst to them, they, through God, played a major part in the formulation of this book.

Therefore, within this volume is a collection of 92 poems. Some are from my personal experiences and others are from yours. We are all connected.

This Cacophony

Uncouth we appear to be. This cacophony.
Unrelated, a compilation of different
colors, ideas and styles.
To the naked eye, voices mixed in a clamor:
loud, disillusioned and confused.
Yet, in truth, against all odds,
this cacophony semi-united.
Disagreeable we appear to be,
unable to relate, yet still we procreate.
Since the beginning of time,
since we became entwined,
through tribal aggression envious backbiting infighting.
We appear to lack refinement and cohesiveness.
This cacophony.
Look deeper and you will see
the beauty, the lack of fuss,
the underlying trust,
the ability to hold it together
in inclement weather. This cacophony.
Ever since, we learned to dine or to keep time.
Once we learned to sit in some semblance of peace,
this cacophony has learned to teach,
to impart our thoughts through words and deeds.
This cacophony has become brothers.
We have fought. We have torn apart at times
our brother's heart. Yet in the mix of the mire,
within the essence of our beings, we stand
side by side. This cacophony.
Think you that we cannot get along.

Yet, this cacophony has climbed mountains,
built bridges. This rabble has come together,
aided enemies during catastrophic manifestations,
in the face of natural disasters, foes forgot their woes.
This cacophony has passed on secrets to each other,
vowed never to be told.
This cacophony has bred with each other's daughters
and forged new nations from nothing.
This cacophony, right from the start,
has never really been apart.
Black, White, Red, Yellow.
Every color of the tribe has stayed alive.
This cacophony throughout time,
during wars, famines, tidal waves, earthquakes,
fires and floods, in gains and major pains, still stands together.
    This Cacophony, Us.

Life

Avant-garde

Her radical techniques were
Avant-garde. She certainly put
those old boys to the test. The way
she conducted business was fresh.
It would bring their antiquated
methods to a finish. Thus, the old
regime became relentless in trying
to find ways and means to eradicate
her very being. However, they did not
understand, she wasn't a man.
Therefore, the ways they planned would not
stand. They did not know, she was
taught by a master, which made her
work faster and smarter than them.
Therefore, all their expressions of
dismay could not sway the powers
that be, or stop the way she attacked
the front each day. In the end she
became their boss, regardless of the
games, they still lost.

At Face Value

The quintessential setting,
unequaled! The exclusive
home, magnificent! The
pinnacle of wondrous living.
Charter members of the yacht
club, both seaworthy at best!
In the wealthiest community.
On the Peninsula, by the course!
Unrivaled, in his field! Charity,
her deal! The exquisite paintings
in the gallery, dramatic stone
creations! Still, their life
was empty. Custom love songs
written for them! Complementing
each other, at social events.
However, under exceptional lighting
while dining, no words were spoken!
It was a token! They went to separate
rooms, separate beds! Only him and
her knew their marriage was dead!

Dad's Chair

The arms were worn out in the
spot where elbows would be.
The high back leaned to the right.
One of the legs was just
stuck on with glue.

It was daddy's chair.

When he was away, we would play
in it. I would dream of being he,
smoking and laughing at the TV.

However, when he was home it was
his and his alone!

Waiting for Dad

I remember waiting for him.
Sitting by the door. Waiting.
The knob would turn,
and it would be he.
His face exuded compassion
and love.
He always gave me Cracker Jacks.
I loved him even more,
each time he walked in the door.

I would take a nap with him,
watch him sleep. Wanting to grow
and mature as he. His muscles made
mine look like little bumps.
He always gentle, with mother.
I hit my sister once. He told me
never hit a woman again. I abide
still to this day, to what he did.
Not what he said!

Darkness Overcomes Me

Darkness is here inside me.
I see no sun I hear no birds.
I feel only dread and terror.
Lunacy runs amuck through my
being in a murderous frenzy.
My soul is lost somewhere
in time. Somewhere in days
of youth, I lost my way.
I took this wicked path.
Is it too late to travel
the road of sanity?
To whom can I turn?
Whom can I trust?
Myself? NO!
Committees of devils
dance in my mind nightly.
Fever and suffering overcome
me. I am lost.

Earth Crying, Dying

It is the rain falling, calling.
Calling to the universe begging,
pleading. Help! I am dying, I am
crying. Sending forth my tears
into the wind. My children do not
see what they do to me.
Are they unconscious of the confusion,
the disillusion of oil spills on me?
Can't they see? It was not meant
for me to house within my bosom
bombs, things of destruction.
Am I falling from grace?
Do not they understand the demand
they place on me, if simple rainforests
cease to be? What of the tree, what
of the grass each time the gun flash?
What of the misuse of my land,
the building of cities on quick sand?
Tears flow from me. Children of the
Earth wake up and see what you do to me.

Failed Attempt

One more chance.
One more chance.
For love!
That's what she thought.

Lily would take one more cruise.
This time. This time!
She would find the man
of her dreams.
She prepared as before.
The right outfits. She charted the
dinners, the dancing, the days on
deck in the sun.
However, it was another,
failed attempt.
No man could fill her request.
No man could fit the build; no
man would step up to the plate.
For Lily it was just too late.

Family Dinner

Cocktails before dinner.
Katrina drunk, blowing
hot smelly liquor in my face.
Bob smoking a cigar, its
ambience woody, leaving traces
of smoke that made you choke.
Upon entering the dining room,
each scrambled to the usual chair.
Uncle Burt sat next to Lisa.
I think he gained something from
her by osmosis, don't know what.
I placed between Mom and him.
I disliked him, I despised him.
This once a year function, made
painful by mother's insistence,
was as always going downhill.
Then it occurred, someone asked,
"What have you been doing all
year?" And hell began, once again.

Family Fiber

Two families with strong fiber.
I mean backbone! Her folks
came to Ellis Island. Working in
New York, labor! His, deep-rooted
in Alabama. Blackfoot mixed in
somewhere. Both worked hard.
Taking care of each other,
no matter the issue, no matter the
fight! He knew his fiancée and he
would make it. Married in 53,
bearing child in 54.
No sabbaticals, vacations from
their relations. Through the
humdrum, his encounters, her
mistakes. They were entangled,
petrified in marriage.
Due to lineage and values. They
would stay together! Literally,
until death they do part.

The Grocery List

He would sit down, grab a sheet
of paper and write
the same things over and over,
each week year after year
milk, eggs, bacon
cookies
T.V. dinners (chicken, turkey,
Salisbury steaks)
pop, pop corn
ice cream sandwiches
yogurt
lettuce
hot sauce
lunch meat
garbage bags, bleach
dishwashing liquid

This was his list.
This was his lot,
this was his life.

The Periodicals

The bi-yearly visit to town.
With it came reason to continue!
He would be picking up the
massive stack of periodicals.
For six months, anticipation
would build. This spring was
especially important! His chance,
to read of the Sarong, his
only reminder of the Pacific.
A piece on the Fishwife (vulgar to
her husband and why). A Medical
Journal, with a provoking article.
(Movable folds of the eyelid).
Moreover, plans for a new Concourse
at Fairbanks Airport.
As winter ended however, he would
gravitate to magazines devoted
to self-containment. He was after all,
still alone, after all these years.

I Left My Mark

I walk through the snow, watching it
glisten and sparkle.
No one had trodden this path before.
No one stepped this way, this day.
Those hyperbaric flakes under my feet.
I take each step in anticipation
of the sound, "crunch", "crunch"!
The white powder under pressure.
Nevertheless, my pressure is not as great as the compact,
compiling flakes.
The stacks, on top of stacks, waiting.
These flakes not able to foresee
there will be no more, tonight.
Not knowing as the thermometer rises
there will be no trace of my steps, my journey across this
place.
The only place
that for a day I could leave my visible mark, my mantra.

In Natchez

As I sat at the antebellum house
thinking of my ancestors baking
in the sun, working plantations.
Visions of them running towards
swamps to escape pure suffering
came to me. Visions of Natchez
where the French came in 1716.
Did they know that my people
would not be free? Would not
be free until Civil War and
Emancipation came, then
Reconstruction. Could they
conceive descendants of Africa
on street corners dealing dope
and death! For what? A thick gold
chain. More importantly, did I
understand the symbolism?
Gold chains, replacing rusty
ones worn during Middle Passage.

Lean Not On Your Own Understanding

I finally know why. There are
wondrous, superfluous matters.
Secrets beyond minimal grasp.
Things of birth, life, death.
The burrowing of the ant.
Cavalcades of celestial bodies
impossible to censure. What do
I know? Can I explain the
Menderes River, its winding
course? Percentile of bees
to produce honey? After years in
Germany, I know nothing of the
mystery or magic of the Rune.
How is it allowable to percolate
so little of the Universe? All a
resonance of cause and effect.
Perfection not my quality. Epicenters,
Godly calls. My concern? I therefore
digress and defer, yield. I surrender
to the MASTER and CREATOR.

Manifesto of Youth

The young man said,
"I will heal the
sick, feed the poor.
I will give of myself to
all my brothers.
I will be a transmitter
of hope and joy.
I will comfort the elderly.
I will protect all creatures
on God's green earth."

However, he was young,
he could not understand that
to accomplish such things,
you must be one hell of a man!
You have to practice
every day to stay that way.
Therefore, time elapsed and
his simple Manifesto
simply Collapsed.

Metamorphosis

Not only the insect world,
we too, have Metamorphosis!
From womb, to tomb like a
cocoon-filled plant. We change
from demure selves to
dependent/independent persona.
Only the observant eye may
see, discern the change!
Like the centipede,
with each segment of our lives,
we conform and configure. Our souls
on a most wonderful hypnotic
journey as the Butterfly. You
and I, giddy when young, become
stern as the years pass! Some
never eject from the silk and
remain encased. Some become
emasculated in sour ideas,
beliefs and behaviors. Have
you grown Wings?

Misunderstood

My words twisted,
thoughts misinterpreted.

Heart of mine, Misunderstood!

All resounding of my voice,
become conditions of astasia.
My yes will not stand, my no gives
no demand.
An assortment of assumptions, my
requests have become.

Heart of mine, Misunderstood!

Discern what I say, listen to the
way the way the words are sent
forth. Then you will know, then
you will feel.

Heart of mine, Misunderstood!

My Heart Went Out That Night! (Roaming Bogotá)

Miserably hot, a steamy haze rose
from black gravel, attributes of
torrent rain. Temperatures hovered
around 105. Beads of sweat slid
down my forehead into my mouth,
leaving a salty taste. Visions of sour
Margaritas floated in a sensory manner.
I sat at café, miles from the city, museums,
and government buildings. Away from the
bull fights of Santmaria. It was there
I noticed a boy. His eyes big, sunken, hollow.
Insect bites on his legs and arms.
Out the corner of my eye, I watched him.
He, tattered, his shoes overrun.
Hair matted a maple color.
Sickened was I watching him search for food.
He surveyed intrinsic items, which might
be traded. How could this be? A child
roaming, living on the streets!
A child without love or compassion.
A child without material satisfaction.
This was not a natural reaction.
Overly saddened by his plight, I cried!
Tears came to my eyes.
Not understanding how we could, would allow,
such a travesty within earth's gravity.
Could this be because of me, did my

listless humanity, contribute to this malady?
A child eating from the streets like a beast!
My heart went out that night witnessing
his plight, his blight.
Thus, the following day I took, I whisked him away.
Now he smiles. He is warm, fed and has a bed.
Each night at home, I read him poems,
tuck him in.
Then I ask my maker to insure,
that he never endures
such trials again.
That he never be alone on his own!

Not When It Comes To Momma

A woman of feministic mind,
way ahead of her time.
Far advanced in political life,
womens rights.
Able to step outside of self,
able to address complex issues
without bias, without prejudice.
But not when it came to momma.
Momma must remain the same.
Pasted in apron, pristine,
unspoiled. As when daddy was
there. When Ms. Progressive was
a little girl, with hair in
frizzy little curls, jumping on
Po-go stick, lying in bed sick.
Momma must not date, be in stride
with current tides. Momma must
stay back in the days of
childhood play. Therefore, in her mind
momma had no choice, no voice.

Separatism

The nationalist group seemed to
have all their stuff in order.
Ideas and conceptions made sense to
me! Why not? After all, should not
all people's rights be respected?
They advocated self-government,
economic power and better conditions!
Yea!

However, what I did not see, eluded
me. It was really about hate, escape,
disgrace of a particular race. Buddy,
I cannot be involved in this, for any
case or cause. It would place a bind
on me, in me, through me. Nah, I seek
to be free. Free from limitation of
spirit and chains of prejudice. My soul
aches for the oneness of it all. This
was not it, no way, no how! Therefore, I
separated myself.

Is This Deep or What

The Deep South seemed like
deep space. Reason. Because of
the deep dark color of my face,
I was in some deep water. So,
to get out of this deep-freeze,
I had to deepen my deep voice
and deeply dig down to convince
this deeply patriotic group that
I was not a deep-sea diver.
I was in deep cover, on a covert
mission for the government.
I had been deeply, laid
in the midst of their deeply white
supremacist group, to prove that
they were not deeply responsible
for a bombing that they had not
committed. All this to insure I was
not deep-sixed. In addition, that they were not
placed in deep Shit. They would have
to deeply believe me and set me free.

Shallow Man

He was a shallow man,
carried his pride in his hand.
Open-minded he could not be
fore he refused to see
the equality of humanity.
A Bigot was he, taught that
way from the very first day.
Taught by his father to
disrespect others, to shut out
brothers of other earthly mothers.
Of course, this caused his demise,
not to anybody's surprise.
You see he was shot by one of
his own while alone at home.
The police who responded
were not of his ethnic code.
He refused to open the door,
thus he died
right there on the floor!
Shallow was he, what about thee?

She Walks the Line

Walking the fine line,
a line between Black and White.
White in the daylight, black and
wild at night! Didn't know what
she wanted to be, this way she
would never be free!
Accepted in the White business
world, this in-between girl.
Uninhibited in the Black, not
judged or scrutinized, not required
to be refined when she dined.
However, torment in her mind certainly
increased with time. Torn between
two worlds kept her head in a swirl.
One day a choice she must make, heart
it will take. White or Black what
will she be?
Well, let us wait and see.

Encore

Everyday, preparation for her role.
Makeup and nails applied meticulously.
Blow-dry the hair, select the
right outfit. Purse matching
as only she knew how! The right
coat, jacket or sweater, depending
on conditions. Last on the list,
rings, earrings and watch. They set
the tone, the mood.

Only after such details could the
Encore begin. And the crowd
wanted more. The Taxi Driver,
the Doorman, the Newspaper guy.
Her boss made extra
visits to her office.
Everyone, Everyday, wanted more!
And she would always re-appear.
The curtain would always re-open.

Boutique

She sold alligator, ostrich
and a most precious lizard line.
She would dress for success
everyday. Hoping, praying,
this day would be the day!
The day that Someone would
notice the small bag, the one
she designed! The one in the corner.
She dreamed of her own line.
She looked in the mirror each
morning and repeated to self.
"That's my design, my line"!
She would wait and anticipate the
response, "Your line is fine".
And of course, she would
reply, "I have over 100 styles,
available in 100 colors".
But like yesterday, this was not
the day for expectations
to be met, not yet!

Mad Man

He stood in the streets
Preaching and Teaching.
As we passed by, pointing
his fingers, they always
seemed to linger. We avoided
his remarks of fire and
brimstone. His words went
straight to our bones. Even
his tone wouldn't leave us alone.
He spoke of how we must change.
How life was meaningful,
that we all should be ashamed.
His words brought us Pain! WHY?
Because, he was really SANE!
He knew we knew life was no
game! Nevertheless, we played it just
the same. Carefree and Careless.
That is why his words left us
in a peculiar fury, frenzy and DISTRESS!
He made us feel our own MESS!

The Sun Also Shines

I sat in my room, full of doom
and gloom. Dark clouds passing
by the window. Drops of rain
pendant size falling.
Depression calling. Yet one of
her isms has reminded me
that the sun also shines.
That it shines on thee and me.
It shines on mountains and valleys.
It shines on streams and rivers.
The ghost of her smile beckoned
me, to recall that previous fall
when the wind blew the leaves
around the trees and the sun was
shining on mother earth and her
children. She, not in arms reach,
conjured up the sun shining on the
masses beaming rejuvenation, causing
perspicacious perspiration.

The Violin

It hypnotizes with waves of
beauty, this European instrument,
14 inches, crafted by hand.
Delegating chordophonic melodic
tunes that echo as strings
vibrate. Legato to Pizzicato
from wood, string and fingerboard.
I close my eyes and dream of
supreme sounds that overtake my
soul. I envision Orchestra, Jazz,
Bluegrass, as it recoils
from magnificent bridge and belly.
Mystery and clarity causes me
to be ensnared by faces of young
and old, on chin rest. I gallivant
in rooms with perfectionist
practicing hours. Rooms over-run
by fingers, sending range and volumes
of heavenly notes. Causing peace.

The Artist

He would stroke his goatee,
contemplating the next stroke of
the brush. He studied others,
mothers and brothers. I passed
him by, wanting to receive a
glimpse of his heavenly work.
His paintings captured my spirit.
His work on canvas mercurial.
One day shadowy, the next almost
maniacal and twisted. Yet still,
an innocence and subtle underlying
transparency accompanied each piece.
He an Artiste, a performer of the
Arts. Don't know if his work will
hang in The Musee due Louvre.
In moments of solitude and
introspective revolution and
revelation they do however, hang in my mind.

Volume

Turn it down! Why do you play it so loud?
Can't you hear, are not the words clear?
I can't allow that banging in my ear.
My hearing is too dear, just like my
sight. My life would be a fright,
if I could not hear! The train at
night. Those banging boxes from
the young boys, passing by in their
fast toys. The babies crying for milk
as their mothers pay them no mind.
That honking horn at three in the morn.
The news about the killings in Africa,
suicide bombings.
On second thought, turn the volume
all the way up. Now it is clear!
Play that music in my ear. Then I
will not have to think about the world
being in the sink. "Blast that volume
to escape torturous planetary rape"!

Thick Lips

Do my Thick Lips offend THEE?
Does the deep voice that echoes
outward cause concern?
Hate?
Cause I not look like THEE?
At one time, these Thick Lips
offended even ME!
Because I did not know whom
I wanted to BE!
Think I did not like ME!
Was under the misconception I
would never be FREE.
But now, I Proudly say.
"These Thick Lips belong to ME,
Black Man I AM,
Black Man I WILL BE.
There is NOTHING WRONG
WITH ME! Transplanted African King,
That would be ME!"

What Ever Happened to the Milkman?

You would come in a white suit.
I would see you each morning.
Eggs, cheese, milk left by the
door. Where did you go, where could
you be?
The innocence of your day beckons me.
Can't you come back for me to see?
Can't we relax?
Can't we eat together as a family
at the table once more! Must we at
night lock our doors? Each time we
hear those shots, do we have to lie
on the floor?
Milkman, please come back to my
door. I much preferred life when it
was a bore. I harken to the days
of your innocence once more.
When you disappeared, so did we.
It is plain to see.
Oh Milkman come back, we need thee!

What If Mankind Used The Feminine Side?

We should use the other side
of our brains. State of War
would be no more, men
and women would not die!
The world would be better.
Anger, hate would disappear.
We would relate, get some
faith, stop the hate.
Peace would happen,
nations would come together.
More would be fed, more
would have beds. Love would
abound, hope would be found.
Oil would be flowing,
churches glowing, cities
thriving instead of dying.
Global warming would not be.
Oh, would we allow this to be?
We all could be Free!

Why

Must we slaughter our animals?
Do we really need what the Seal
has? The things they use to protect them in icy
domain. Can't we forego the
killing of the Whale?
Is the magnificent Tiger
here to appease me?
What of the humongous Elephant,
must we have the tusk? Are God's
creatures only for our pleasure?
To feed, satisfy our innate greed.
To show and tell. I killed this!
I have that! Behold my Trophy on
the wall, the biggest of them all!
Do you like my fur? It would not
look good on her. Would it?
WE, Self-seeking.
Self-satisfying.

A Voice on the Phone

A voice on the phone had this to
say, "This is not normal for me,
but I have to say, I saw you. You
have a presence about you. A kind
of awesome luminous aura surrounds
you. There is something in your eyes.
You have me hypnotized, mesmerized.
You stand erect, walk direct.
You look so fine, you will be mine!
I got your number from a friend,
was hoping to see you again.
Do you think this might be?
May we go on a date? Call me back
before eight."
I called that day, not normal for me.
However, I have to say, it turned out to be
she was the one for me. We just got
married last week, moved to L.A.
Therefore, a voice on the phone led to
a new wife, a new home.

Chivalrous

Appearing unfettered by
events. He, solid in demeanor,
able to pour from decanter
a straight line of brandy.
They watched unbeknownst,
'twas inward he channeled
anger. Soon, he would uncase
the rage within.
You see, he, unschooled in
wicked ways. He unschooled in
deception and deceit.
Nonetheless, he would extract
a most heinous penalty from them.
They who used him as proxy
against My Lady Diane. Used him
to draw her to parley with vipers.
As if in a Pas de deux, interlocking
him in their saber-like scheme.
He would avenge her. He would die
for honor, for valor, for her!

Constrictions

Sea to shore, flower to sun!
Bird to sky, river to lake.
Drawn together, without choice!
A certain natural bonding,
no chance involved!
Connecting, blending as one!
Alas, Me to you!
As grass to earth. Growing from,
conforming! Things unstoppable.
No borders, no boundaries,
no containment possible!
Dare say I, even feasible!
Nothing! Nothing! Will, can, keep us apart!
As rain comes to wind! Music to ears.
These forces cannot be restricted!
Ever moving towards,
joining, interlocking.
A most natural procession!
So too, our love!

Emeralds in Her Eyes

Like the Emerald Isle.
Reminiscent of grass
on a misty morn, as the sun
rises on the meadow
and its upward mobility reaches
above the timberline.
Clear Deep green,
the color of her eyes.
Like fresh printed money
rolling off the press.
Clear Deep green.
She had Emeralds in her eyes.
I only saw her once,
once was enough!
Enough to hear the Songbird.
Enough to conjure up visions of
Rembrandt painting her.
Enough to estimate the effects of
those eyes on so many hearts,
as they had already relegated mine.

South of the Border

Old Blue Eyes sang!
"South of the Border down
Mexico way! That's where I
fell in Love!" Didn't
plan to stay! However, Love
directed my way! She had long
black hair, eyes big like
new money! And Boy OH Boy,
lips sweeter than Honey.
That's why, I gave her
all my money! Got stuck down
here, it sure wasn't Funny!
Couldn't get back, my mind
was a wreck! Each day I say,
What the Heck! I'll lay
here under the sun, drinking
Gin and living in Sin!
South of the Border.

If You Love Me

If you love me, you would not
judge me. That's what she said,
as I hung my head. Furthermore,
if you love me, you would not
hurt me, or push me away.
If you love me, you would not
put unrealistic expectations
on me. You would accept me
for who I am.
Be my friend, honor and
respect me, not neglect me.
If you love me, these things
you would do! Protect me,
encourage me, uplift me.
Honest you would be to me,
faithful and true.
If you love me, these attributes
would exude from you!

How Could I Let Her Get Away?

I ponder on this, day in and day out.
Was I neglectful or negative in any way?
Did I not play or pay?
Did I abuse her in any way?
Did I say, good morning or good night?
Did I let her out of my sight?
Did I kiss her at night, did I tuck her in?
Was I her friend?
Did I leave her alone too long?
How long would I stay gone?
Did we have fun, or was I a man on the run?
Did I pray for us at night?
Did I always think I was right?
I ask myself each and every night!
Why did she run away?
Why did not she stay?
I must get on with my life!
Can't dwell on her flight.

How Will You Know?

A love for you is in this world.
It can pass you by if you don't
have an open eye.
The one for you can slip away,
never to return for another day.
Here are some things you can
do to remain open to the love
that is just for you!
When you meet someone, right from
the start, have an open mind and an
open heart. Ask yourself, could this
be the one and only one for me?
Look into their eyes, you should be
able to see, what God has stored
inside. You will see, if you look
deep, deep down into their eyes.
Always listen to what they say.
If they are foolish, it will be
revealed that first day, right away!
If you do these things, you will know.

How Many Hearts

How many hearts have you broken?
How many hearts have you
disregarded as mere tokens?
How many hearts have you torn
apart, walked away from?
Leaving someone to fend
on his or her own in disrepair alone.
Your child-like mentality seems
to keep you from reality.
People's hearts aren't easy to
mend. Sometimes it's hard to
find that life long romantic
friend.
You do not care, you say it does not
matter. You will live and love,
kiss and tell, walk over those
who have pledged allegiance to you.
You fool, this is the reason
so many hate you.

Sheers at the Window

Entranced each night at 12:02.
Only a silhouette I glimpse
upon, as she passes sheers in
the window. Long and lean,
she appears to be fit and trim.
I, captivated by the charm of
her steps. Her shadow transparent,
Geisha-like sensuous!

Come what may each day, come
seismic scenarios, I will endure,
just to have a glance, an
ingathering of her beauty.
The innocence of her image
smothers out the pain of
loneliness. She teases me into
a hypnotic state. All worthwhile
as she brings a smile to the end
of every gut wrenching day.

I Saw a Heron

Walking on the beach,
I saw a heron!
It had long legs, long neck
and a long bill. It somehow
took me to the day I met her.

Yes, it reminded me of her.
She was like a heron to me,
frail, evasive, extraordinary.
She had a melodious walk.
I envisioned her on the beach,
in the sand with no shoes.
She too seemed inept, but
as the heron, able to fly.
Able to catch men's eyes, break
their hearts and make them cry.
And as with her, I wanted to cage it,
to clip its wings.
Why was the hunter still in me?

If I

If I could make the rivers flow,
catch a falling star, cause
the rain to fall or wind to blow
I would, for you!

If I could make the sun rise and set,
or cause life to have no regrets,
I would, for you!

If I could make mountains come
alive, or conceptualize prose
and poem, I would, for you!

If I could transverse the universe,
deport or banish yesterday, or cause
icebergs to sway, I would, for you!
Fore, Love has come my way. And if
these powers I did possess,
If I could, I would, for you!

If Love Comes Your Way

If love comes your way,
it will tell you what to say.
Love will have its way.
It will tell you what to do.
Love will make a fool of you.
It will direct you.
Love will make you quake,
make you beg for a simple date.
It will cause you to want, to ache
for them. Love is not your friend.
Love will cause no regard for self.
It will have you put self-respect
on the shelf. Love is for itself!
It will make you high, take you low.
And when you fall in love many nights,
you will crawl into a fetal ball.
Love cares nothing for you,
this is what love will do.
If love comes your way, you will play,
you will have absolutely nothing to say.

Internet Affair

We would get together
without getting together,
if you know what I mean!
As the Beatniks
would say, "It was a most
crazy scene".
Each night I would run to the
screen the tube, to get my
daily fix from her.
We shared our dreams and hopes,
the scope of our existence.
Then, one night I rushed to
the screen, to my new
obsession. To make my nightly
confession! But, Nothing,
I mean Nothing! Now, each
night I roam the net, trying
to find my hyper-space mate!

The Matchmaker

She arranged dates. She would,
coordinate intricate rendezvous.
She could put them together
without haste. 99.9% of her charges
were married and most satisfied.
Yes, her skills were verified!
Nevertheless, she was terrified.
Each night, ice cream and TV,
was all she would see. No kisses,
no hugs. Only tears and pain.
Her life would always be
the same. Love for her pure
rejection, no affection. Her
personal connections were in vain.
Each night she slept with Teddy Bear.
This plight was hers alone to bear.
Her inner turmoil beyond compare.
Reason? She snored and her toes
had hair like a big black Bear!

Intellectual

He an intellectual.
Matters pending thought,
he pondered upon each day.
Engrossed was he with hepatica.
Thus, herbs as of buttercups he
would watch. Seeking out their
bluish color became pastime.
However, it was the sacred art of love,
he could not discern mentally.
He could not understand why,
no woman had he.
To put it in proper primary
priority in his rapid moving
logical head, he surrendered or
yielded to the fact that he was
not your best looking chap.
Therefore, he choked on diet of
massive prepositions and nouns.
Pictures of Egyptian sphinxes
became his decimated love life.

It Must Be

This must be a dream!
It cannot be real, this
wonderful way I feel! Never
before has my heart walked
through this door! I prayed
young, this day would come!

Years went by, memories
and pain! A passing refrain,
remaining the same! Then
you came! How can
I explain! My attempts
would be in vain!
No collection of phrases or
sonnets in masterful arrangements
can express my heart's containments
You are my wildest, figuratively
induced elastic, impossible, dream!
May I never wake
from this dream-engaged stage!

Keepsake

He had it in a box,
under the bed, locked!
Within it sentiments, secrets
prevailed. Things he
didn't want anyone to know!
A knife from the 3rd grade,
a card he had made. A lock
of her fair hair. Therefore, each night
in the moonlight, he would
open it up, and cry. The pain
inside never would subside.
The love he lost, because he
refused to toss out old
ideas and fears! Consequently,
each night ended in tears!
Him peering at the box of memorable
things. Things he chose not to forget
of the woman he met, and would
always regret not taking the train
that day, so long ago!

The Shoe

He tripped on it, a shoe
lying precariously in the way.
You see, he was prone to lapse,
into visual holograms.
One might think him high, not
the case. He just propelled
self into his own world. And what
a world! He saw her in the shoe.
She, 110 pounds, thin, delicate,
fragile. Just the kind of woman
he adored. He saw himself at
her door. They went dancing,
the tango and various
configurations of ballroom style,
engaged in wonderful conversation.
Subjects, wine and absolution of
past derelictions. They embraced,
kissed, she left.

Love Me

Can you love me? Will you
overlook my faults? Can I
be myself with you? May I
uncover? Try to (in-to-me-
you-see)! The mistakes I
make may abound. I won't
comb my hair! Sometimes
I am a lout and lovelorn!
I can be a lion brave and
true. On other days, I may
need to hide behind you!
And when all is said and done, if you
take me as I am, I will be
your friend! I will hold you
up, lift your spirit! Take
you as you are! Like me,
wanting love, to be cherished,
accepted.

Love Retreat from Me

You are too painful. Retreat from me!
You are excused, leave my presence!
Your ways are too stern, your pins
too sharp. Your smile too devious.
Love, your grasp is too tight.
You take the life from me.
You cause me to want, to need.
I don't normally act this way.
You cause me to come clean,
be honest and upright.
You bring forth tears. At dusk, you
cause me to ache. You are too cruel!
For the one I love, loves me not.
The one I love, aches for me not.
The one I cry for, sheds no tear
for me. She has no emotionalisms
towards me either way. She knows not
that my heart exscinds all others.
Love retreat, go away now, Please.

Marry Me!

Marry Me, Be my wife.
Share with me the strife's
of life. The joys, the pains,
even the insane.
Life may get crazy, we may
end up with babies.
But with you as my wife,
it will be alright.
Please, assume the position at
my side, not in front, nor behind.
Walk with me stride by stride,
handling the tides of life, all
will be joy with you as my wife.
Be the commentator of my passions,
keep me on the narrow path. Push
me if you must, remember it will
be about us. Hold my hand walking
towards our goals. A spectacular
future do I behold and foresee.
If you will only Marry Me!

The Answer

Yes, I will love you all of
my life. I will hold you
up if you fall. I will help
you stand tall.
I will be myself with you
honest, open and true.
If we get in a rut, I will
lift us up. I will accept you,
as you are, placing no unreal
expectation on our relation.
I'd be most happy to have your
babies, walk beside you during
the pain and the rain.
I will push you if I must,
always remembering it is
about us.
So, to answer your question
without further hesitation.
I will be your wife.
Marry thee, and raise our family.

Matters of the Heart

She came to me trembling,
crying, sighing.
She swore, "Never Again!
I won't let him in, I do not
deserve to be treated this way."

This not being the first time
and I suspected not the last.
I listened.
I laid her head upon my lap.
I wiped her tears.
I told her I loved her.
And as I always do, I informed her
"Matters of your heart are
up to you!"
Then just as each and every day,
after the session of her personal
confession, I sent her on her way,
waiting to open the door another day.

Mental

Sometimes my mind goes.
I think of far, far away places.
I disoblige against myself. What
I want to do, I do not do.
I am but a marionette in the palm
of my subconscious. Painting a picture
without control of the brush.
Statements are not foregone,
but spontaneous.

All that can bring me back to reality
is your voice. The sweet, melodic,
sound takes me from melancholia.
Back to life I spring! Ready to
do what must be done. Ready to
handle the coming tides of mid-week.
Fore, it is only Tuesday! I have
four more days to battle myself.

One Million Kisses

One million kisses will I give thee.
A kiss for each second.
A kiss for each day each week.
A kiss for each month each year.
A kiss for the summer. A kiss for
the winter. A kiss for the spring.
A kiss for the fall. A kiss for
the darkness, for the light.
A kiss for the sun, the moon,
the stars. A kiss for each smile,
each tear, each fear. A kiss for
your pains and your gains.
A kiss for her, for him, for them.
A kiss for your mother, your father.
A kiss for the babies.
A kiss for this. A kiss for that.
A kiss for here. A kiss for there.
A kiss for me for you. A kiss for
something. A kiss for nothing.
One million kisses will I give thee.

Out of the Rain

In Morocco, I began to grow,
felt sorry for self no-more.

On to Berlin, there
became my friend once again,
ceased to beat up on me!

By the time Paris came around
a new faith was found!
I could live again; I could feel
the pain, release the strife.
Yes, the rain is gone,
better days on the horizon.

Two years it has been.
No human touch no need for lust.
But, now I am ready, I look forward
again to life, to love, to pain,
to pleasure.
Possibly, even more rain.

Piece de resistance

Making love to you is the
"Piece de resistance" It is
the apex, of day and night. Making
love to you is charity to my
heart. Making love to you is a
dream come true.
What can compare?
A sunset? A rainbow? The morning dew?
It is a Holy Sacrament, the rushing
of all sensual conceptions. Making
love to you is the advent of my
Soul! It is the picturesque,
account of all things wondrous!
Making love to you is magic!
The creamery of my mind. It takes
me Higher! It is the involution of
my being. It is the permanent,
joining of the stars. It is the
Sherbet filled dessert of my Universe!

Tormented

I met her on a sunny day. Her eyes
seemed so sad. She tried to smile,
but I could see.
She was tormented!
I thought that it would be alright.
Alright, cause I had love in sight!
I loved her best I could. I prayed
for us, I prayed each night for love
to find a way. Only there was nothing
I could do.
Fore, alas she was tormented!
Tormented and tortured by loves,
of past permissions. Some days
were better than others. On many
occasions we laughed, smiled, loved
and laid. But, alas she was tormented!
I catered her, bathed her, kissed her,
loved her. I cried with her. Cried for
her. But alas, she was tormented!

Post Traumatic Stress

Now I stand with nothing.
I could do or say nothing
to brighten up her day.
No song I sang.
No joke I told,
could lift her veil of pain!

So, I submitted to insane things,
projected from her mind. Hectic
illusions she brought forth.
Persuading myself, that love
would prevail. I suppose
she loved me best she
could! She gave me all she could.

But now, I stand because of this,
as consequence of my quick fix,
behind the tactics, I injected,
Post Traumatic, Insane and Neglected.

Ready

The twist and turns of time,
constantly remained on my mind,
causing the ensuing years,
to end in fears. I kept myself
literally in tears. I stopped
the progress of love's calling.
I became impeded, causing all
previous encounters to be
corrupted, nonproductive.
Love's natural flow was not a
go. Thus inept was I, obstructed,
paused from the "Love Clause".
My self-restrictive provisional
mind ensured me to end up
empty-handed, sitting alone and
severely self-reprimanded.

But now I'm ready! The inquisitions
from within beckons me. I am sick
of being alone, on my own.

Shadows of the Heart

When I met her,
she informed me,
there were shadows in her heart.
I asked, "What do you mean?"
She said, "Places where there
is no light. Places left dark by
past relationships. Spaces no
man can fill. Spaces dormant,
dead, dimmed by rejection and lies.
Places where love once dwelled."

Now only craters that cloister
remain. Crying she spilled
out the pain of yester-year.
Of how man after man,
had pummeled and purged her heart.
So now, I could never have a
chance to shine my light inside.
I hung my head, hating men I never knew!

She Was a Concubine in Her Mind

We made love each day. She saw
this the only way to be mine.
I attempted to reassure her, twas'
her entire being I see. How she
was more than a love toy to me. I
informed her of a life we might
have in store. Reiterating she was
no bore. But somewhere back in time,
men put misinformation in her mind.
Mistakenly she bought into it,
the lie that her body twas' her gift.
A travesty for all she met.
I would tell her she did not belong
to me, that her heart was free. I
even asked her to marry me! But so
convinced was she, that she
continued to jump in beds. I tried
to convince her it was all in her
head. She refused to believe me,
thus remaining a concubine instead.

Sinful

It was sinful, it was shameful.
It was not a game, it included no fame.
My mind has never been the same!
We met, we kissed, we joined ourselves.
Then we parted!
It was sinful, it was fun, it was lust.
It was painful, it was playful.
It was fast, it was slow.
It was OH! So sinful, so dirty, so cavalier, so carefree!
It was dangerous, it was focused.
It was a flutter, it was felonious, punishable.
It was euphoric, it was dreadful, distasteful!
It was prophetic, it was rustic.
That meeting sabotaged my soul!
You were a saboteur, you were in control.
Will you please come back?
And give me some more!

Take Me to Mary's Grave

Take me there
I need to see.
I will not stare
tis where I need to be.
Near her resting site,
seeking, wanting.
Those walks at night,
soul pleading, taunting.
Eyes digging into ground,
hoping, praying.
To hear her voice, her sound,
to touch her as she is lying.
Never shall I gaze again
upon her face.
She is but a haze.
Earth and I have lost her grace.
To hold again my love,
my friend, my dove.
Take me to Mary's grave, please!
I was her slave, twill put me at ease!

That Kiss

Stamped on my memory,
planted in my heart,
intertwined with my mind,
interwoven in my soul.

That kiss, not as any other.
Deep, wet, long, flirtatious.
Amorous it was.

That kiss sent visions of marriage,
babies, a house on the hill. It sent
chills up and down my spine.
It caused an emotional effect like
never before. It made me want more!

Yes, that kiss at that door that
night was out of this world.
It was universal, it was
transcontinental. It was magical.
It has no equal. It needs a sequel!

The Center of My Universe

This verse, directed to, composed
for YOU! The one who infiltrates
my dreams each night.
The one I desire, admire, pray to
acquire. The one I acquiesce to.
The one I aspire, in chiffon
on my bed. That one with elegance,
tenderness. The one I will
live with and love.
That one who holds the keys to
the mansions of my heart. That
one from whom I will never part.
"Where are you?"
Without you, my life is dark, bleak.
My soul has no contour, color or
contrast! My Being naught. There is
nothing to eat or drink. I am in a
famine. Come to me, I beseech thee!

The Garden

You didn't think I had a garden?
That is what I asked her! "Yes,
you are right, didn't take you
for the type!" So I said come
with me and see. Took her hand,
led her to my Garden Land. When,
she saw herbs and shrubs neatly
trimmed I knew I had her then!
I showed her Pink Mallows.
Explained the Dahlias, the colors
yellow, orange, red, a most
delightful purple. I went on
about the Strawflower
(Helechrysum), about their height!
She was into the Zinnias. I informed
her; they were hybrid and grow to
twenty inches. Then, off to my pride and joy the
Calendula or Pot Marigolds!
That is of course, when I proposed!

These Three Things

A taste of your lips,
just one last deep wet kiss.
A look in your eyes,
before our long goodbye.
A touch of your hand,
to remind me I'm your man.
These three things I forge from thee.
These three things will keep me free.
These three things will hold me tight,
close to your bosom on cold winter
nights.
So beyond the horizon I shall part.
Far away from thee, my love, my heart.
But as I am away from your smile,
your grace, your beautiful face, we
shall not be apart. Fore these three
things, I charter from thee.
They are the things that will keep me
next to thee.
Even as I travel far across the sea.

Until The Sun Shines No More

For a Millennium. Until the sun
shines no more. Until the stars
fall from the sky. Her love for
me would never die. Until there
were no more flowers.
She would have affection for me.
She bequeathed her heart,
to me forever on that day.
Somehow, we became disconnected;
things fell apart, into the sea of
nothingness. Just as she said,
the sun shines no longer.
The stars have fallen from the sky.
And sad to say, all the flowers
met their demise. Clairvoyant she
must be, to see what would be.
My world gone my heart torn.
My soul broken into pieces!

While You Were Out

Oh,
while you were out,
the lights were turned off.
The car repossessed.
The yard became a mess.

While you were gone,
they turned off the phone.
And, guess what?
You no longer have a home.

Oh, by the way, he came into
my life. Now I am his wife!
While you were out and left
me alone.
Now, you're on your own!

Just one more thing, I sold
that cheap ass wedding ring.

Why Won't You Set Me Free?

These are the questions, the
statements she presented to me.

Why won't you let me be free?
Let me fly in the sky?
Why oh why do you keep me
locked up?
Don't you know I will die!
Don't you understand you can't
control me? If you love me,
set me free, allow me to be.
I need not be put under pressure,
don't put me to a faithfulness test.
Have not you learned that yet?
I am not a pet, you are not my
vet, able to fix me, or bring out
my best. I must do that myself.
I must find my own inner wealth.
Of course, I didn't know what to say.
She brought truth to me that day.

Window Conversation

She sat in the window,
staring out, glaring out!
Seeking the past, holding
conversations with self.
Convincing self, that the boy,
the one who comes each morning
by the window, reminded her
of him. Todd! See, it was Todd
who broke her heart! He left her
at the altar! Try as she
would she could not forget.
She went to Istanbul, Europe,
and canals in the Mediterranean.
But every gondola or cafe
reminded her of him. The love
of her life. Day in day out,
so, she sat conversing with
self. As Todd long gone,
taunted her, haunted Her!

Women

Been a lot of places,
seen a lot of things.
Done even more. And YOU have
always been in the picture.
Wherever, whenever, however.

You are my vice, my pain, my joy.
Love YOU and hate YOU at the
same time. YOU give me hopes
and dreams.

YOU give pleasure and rejection.
The highest feeling possible
and the lowest.

YOU are My curse
and blessing. Can't live without
the touch, yet the touch is
sometimes too painful and too Much!

You Make My Rivers Flow

I deemed myself unworthy, counted out
was I. My baby came to inform me
all in my head was just a lie.
She said "You make my rivers flow,
you bring my heart to a glow."
From deep inside, each and every time
I look into your eyes, my being
comes alive. My sacred streams awaken.
My heart begins to quicken, my knees
turn to melted butter, heart goes all
aflutter. The air in my lungs expands
and demands a touch of your sweet hand.
You are truly my man.
Let me make it clear my dear,
"You make my rivers flow!"
A smile came upon my face.
I held my head a little higher.
My soul came out of the mire.
Fore, I surely did not know
that I made my baby's rivers flow.

Spirit

A Storm Is Coming

The horizon is dark,
wind begins to blow, trees
start to structurally shake.
A storm is coming!
Drops of heavy rain appear.
Folks tie down worldly possessions
and close their windows.
Fear and worry looms large around town.
But I won't worry. I won't fret.
Because God is with me, I shall
not get that wet. So, as wind
blows and things are tossed about,
I will stand strong, God has got
my back! As darkness enfolds all,
my faith shall light the way.
Cause I believe and trust the
storm won't come my way.
And if by chance, it does,
with God I'll be OK.

Down on Bended Knees

Knowing the consequences,
down on bended knees,
I come to Thee!
On the days when life is a haze,
and the outlook is gray,
down on bended knees,
I come to Thee!
When the pain is great, and from
it there is no escape,
down on bended knees,
I come to Thee!
When there is nowhere else to go,
when there is no-one else who knows
which way to go, where to turn,
down on bended knees
I come to Thee!
When the wind rushes in and the
storm is at my door,
when my tears saturate the floor,
down on bended knees, I come to Thee!

Dreaming

Oh, I've been dreaming,
dreaming of heaven of hell.
Dreaming of hope of joy,
of pain of sorrow.
Dreaming of a better tomorrow.
Oh, I've been dreaming
of you, of love, of apple pie.
I've been dreaming of monetary
gain, of fame of fortune.
I've been dreaming of losses.
Dreaming of values, convictions
of world religions.
Oh, I've been dreaming of life,
of death. Dreaming of mom,
of dad, of kids, of laughter,
of if there is an everafter.
Dreaming of recanting past reactions.
I've been dreaming of wonders
of midnights alone listening to
thunder. Oh, I've been dreaming...

Father Said

If you remain the same, and stay
on a painful course, happiness won't
be obtained. Most of your life will
be in vain. Fore, change comes
through pain. You see the mind
conceives, the soul believes, the
heart frees. The spirit seeks to
live, not die. This is why when in
pain, the spirit cries for treasures
of the heart. It seeks souls dwelling
in peace those already released.
This, my son, is the soul's way to
calm an internal beast. The soul
seeks the eternal nurse. Need I repeat
this verse? This is what my father
said. I believed him. I kept it in my
head, listened to my heart, adhered
to the things I was told regarding
the soul. I did this all of my life.
The results, less holes, in my soul.

Glacier

From the cruise ship, I met you.
Your mass, your form extending
from high descending below
captured me. You were ever moving,
yet still. Your colours a mix of
octamerous lights. Awe and wonder
overtook my being as I watched.
Fog covered top, gave you the
appearance of an icy God.
The accumulation of ice, of cold,
sent chills through my mortal soul.
With you, I felt joined as one.
Your inner mysteries a shocker
to me. What lay within? As shive
and splinters of your bounty
floated by, a question, what would
a highball taste like surrounded
by you? As ship drifted away, I
stared, as steam rose, I wept.
I would miss you, my friend.

Midnight Prayer

At midnight, each night,
I pray. I pray for the earth
not to give birth to floods and
famine. I pray for the children,
for unwed mothers and
lost fathers.

Each night, at midnight,
I pray, I pray for peace to be
reached. I pray for bombs not to
fall, at all. For rain to
fall, for wind to blow,
for grass to continue
to grow.

At midnight, each night,
I pray for one more day!
At midnight, each night,
I pray, I pray for God to come our way.

Misty Lake

At Misty Lake, she sat in the
morning dew. Tears would appear
in the wells of her eyes. I
thought her praying.
She watched ripples as they
scanned across fog covered deep.
Scrutinizing each bubble from
fish planted by bird-dropped eggs.

She brings serenity my way.
As I, on my way each day to
the chores that I bore. Watch her!
She surreal. Sitting, praying,
swaying, never saying a word.
Butterflies hover over her,
dancing. Trying to divert her.
She never deviates, from her task.
Never!

Nomad

Driving the winding road of life.
Roaming across time and space.
To get away from it all, to escape
reality, morality, finality.
Small town folk welcome me, they
give me smiles and comfort. They
dish out food in ghost town diners,
to line the belly. I am dispatched
to county fairs and one-ring circuses.
I perform, and then collect the scraps
left for my edification. I, Nomad,
wander attempting to find my hamlet,
my home. The faces change, but all
remains the same. I continue my
journey each sunrise, never planting
root. Yet, still the collections of
faces and places give me certain
pleasures when self and I lay down
to rest at night.

Plugged In

A warm sunny day. A cool
breeze upon my face. Smiles
and laughter in the air.
And I was plugged in. Plugged
into the universe. Plugged into
my feelings, the sensitivity of
my fellow man. There was not
a thing my soul was missing.
It was an outstanding day!
I was connected to her and him,
you and yours. My heart full
of compassion, not reaction.
I could smell life itself.
I felt human, I felt good.
I was Plugged In. The world
was once again my friend.
Happy was I, joyous and Free!
Glad to be alive.

Sleep, Shall I Find Thee?

Another turn on yonder clock,
yet one more hour, blending
into previous ones. Eyelids
tired, weary, rendered incapable.
The mind in a perpetual state
of tossing of turning of
yearning for thee, anticipating
dreams, seeking ability to
think of nothing. Evasive
are thou, you, state called
sleep. Where might thou be?
My soul beckons, pleads for
thee. Is it by design or are
there strange talismans to
keep thee away? Does the night
find me unworthy? Tomfoolery
thou bring to me! My pillow I
shall not see. Thou will not
come to me. Alas, another sunrise
sent to taunt me, Woe onto me!

Taking Out Time

Taking out time to work
on self. Gonna take a break from
the dating scene, not ready for
dates, not just yet.
Next time I date, I will be ready.
I will have something substantial
to give. Instead of bringing old
baggage, mess and a boat load of
past lost love regrets.
I think I'll work on me, see how
much better I can be.
Therefore, when I find that one woman
I won't be tripping, won't always
be saying and doing things to have
to be forgiven. Yes! This is what
I'll do, stay away from that scene
until I'm ready, more steady.
But when I come back, look out baby!
I'll be refined, genuine, able to be
a friend, and open to love once again.

The Colosseum

I awaken at the Roman Colosseum, under suspended canopy, repelling sun. I gaze upon beast on way to demise or human feast. Off-white togas encircle me. Sounds of clanging swords of legends echo. This concrete, marble-seated monstrosity imprisons me. I dash between arches. I am locked and lost within the walls of Flavins Amphitheater, in arms reach of madmen marching to death in needless ancient battle. I am caught within the grandeur of Vespasian's and Dormitian's architecture. How can I escape this nightmare? How can I flee 50,000 raging spectators awaiting my destruction? Will this tiered house of Titus be my grave?

The Hand of God

My Momma used to tell me
about the hand of God!
I heard her, but I did not hear her.
I listened, but I didn't Listen.
I went on my merry way, everyday.
Not thinking, just doing.
Not planning, just running.
Then it happened!
I looked up and saw the hand of God!
I mean, I saw the sun before.
The flowers, the trees and such.
But this was a special day, I must say.
The day was brighter, the wind lighter.
My eyes opened to the human race.
The human pace.
The smiles, the tears, the fears.
I was no longer on the run. Life became fun.
I no longer needed my gun!
My Momma used to tell me about the hand of God.
Now, I tell my son.

The Me You Can Not See

From within stillness.
Shooting outwards.
Circles of life.
Reaching towards infinity.
Ever changing.
Molecular, metaphysical.
Without form.
Yet strictly pointing to oneness.
Bringing about purpose.

This soul, my being.
The me you can not see.

The Process

The qualitative and analytical
processes of my mind.
A mystery to me.
Before I make that mistake,
do I hesitate?
Do I determine the
subjective proportions of
outcomes and consequences of
belated actions, transferred
from the cornerstone of the
cortex, the cerebral and
cerebellum-wet hemispheres
of my being?
Or are my thoughts dorsal
ornaments hanging in darkness?
I put forth this question to self.
If reasonable man I be, why not
total sound judgment and piercing
goodness spring from me?
Instead, wishy-washy man I be!

The Unseen

In Temples, Sanctuaries
and Synagogues.
It has been spoken!
In times of turmoil and revelation.
It has been spoken!
In Cathedrals, Mosques
and Seminaries.
It has been spoken!
During prayer and meditation.
The name, the names.
Feared, Awed, Revered!
Shouted, at the highest Mountains,
whispered, by the deepest waters,
the name, the names.
When troubled and low
it has been spoken!
For help, relief and wisdom
when in pain and grief.
It has been spoken! The name, the names.
Of the Unseen...

Wandering Souls

Our souls wander at night
as we sleep.
They try to find peace.
They mix with other souls
seeking the same.

They dance a private dance.
A dance of harmony and contentment,
a most prolific dance,
a dance in the nothingness of
time and space.
They seek solace from the earthly
constraints of the physical.
They seek that which is contrary to
limited enlisted conditions of
conclusive consciousness.
They seek unity of purpose and thought.
That which cannot be realized in
an awakened state. They seek each other.

Well, Well, Well

He we are, at the break of dawn.
Going over our lives, you and I.
Revisiting the past. Checking
over trials, tribulations endured.
The perceivable mistakes
we've made. Those times we were
mealy-mouthed! Like the ostrich
hiding in the sand. Bringing up
irresponsibility's of youth,
encounters of the strange
kind. Vocalizing the hereditary,
irregular concepts and issues
pressed upon us. Placing our moral
sonar on hex-ridden rickshaws,
pulled by shorthanded mentors
given us. Painstakingly, we peer
at the pedigree not received
at birth. Questioning reasons
for being on Earth.

Who Am I?

To myself I retort over and over,
full well knowing the answer.
I am to change, to grow.
I am to make a difference
in a dying world. I am to
heal a soul. My own!

That is who I am!!!!!!!!
A soul seeker, a light
on the path to enlightenment.
But, alas, without my torch,
without my map, I can not lead
others like me. They will not
be able to see.
Therefore, I dig inside. I set
my foolish, foolish pride aside.
I once again begin to look within.
Inside of me deep down within,
is my friend. ME!
I will find HE!

You're Invited

You Are Invited! To an exorcism
of the soul. Mystical, magical
events are yours to behold.
Of the significance of life.
You will see how mediocrity
does not have to be your plight.
You will be changed, transformed
from the norm. You will no longer
be stigmatized. You will be saved
from strangulation and BS
anticipation.
Will you come?
Will you bring an open mind?
You will be taken to a place of
love and perpetual joy.
The fishbowl will break. You will
be able to escape the confines of
moral decay. Yes indeed.
You are invited, to be enlightened!

2759838

Made in the USA